THE UNTAMED WORLD

Bald Eagles

Karen Dudley

RSVP
RAINTREE
STECK-VAUGHN
PUBLISHERS
The Steck-Vaughn Company

Austin, Texas

Published by Raintree Steck-Vaughn Publishers, an imprint of Steck-Vaughn Company.

Library of Congress Cataloging-in-Publication Data
Dudley, Karen.
      Bald eagles / Karen Dudley.
         p.   cm. -- (The untamed world)
      Includes bibliographical references (p. 63) and index.
      Summary: Describes the life, environment, and habits of bald eagles, and the conditions that threaten them with extinction.
      ISBN 0-8172-4571-5
      1. Bald eagle--Juvenile literature. [1. Bald eagle. 2. Eagles.]
I. Title. II. Series.
QL696.F32D83   1998
599.9'43--dc21
                                  97-1271
                                    CIP
                                    AC

Printed and bound in Canada
1234567890 01 00 99 98 97

Project Editor
Lauri Seidlitz

Design and Illustration
Warren Clark

Raintree Steck-Vaughn Publishers Editor
Kathy DeVico

Copy Editors
Janice Parker, Leslie Strudwick

Layout
Chris Bowerman

Consultants
Michael W. Collopy has studied eagles for 20 years. He is Director of the Forest and Rangeland Ecosystem Science Center, U.S. Geological Survey, in Corvallis, Oregon.

Peter Sherrington is a field ornithologist and conservationist who has been studying eagle migration in the Rocky Mountains since 1992.

Acknowledgments
The publisher wishes to thank Warren Rylands for inspiring this series.

Photograph Credits

Corel Corporation: cover, pages 8, 9, 12, 24, 25, 30, 31 left, 31 right, 33, 37, 38, 45, 55, 59, 60, 61; **HawkWatch International**: page 57; **Ivy Images**: page 28 (Don Johnston); **Parks Canada**: page 13 (W. Lynch); **Michael S. Quinton**: pages 11, 16, 18, 36, 41, 42, 43; **Wilf Schurig**: pages 17, 29, 35; **Tom Stack and Associates**: pages 4 (Jeff Foott), 6, 26, 40 (Thomas Kitchin); **U.S. Fish and Wildlife Service**: pages 5, 32 (Norman Nelson), 10 (Lee Emery); **Visuals Unlimited**: pages 7 (Tom J. Ulrich), 14 (Hugh Rose), 20 (Joe McDonald), 21 (David Ellis), 22 (Charlie Heidecker), 23 (David S. Addison), 27 (R. Lindholm), 44 (Kjell B. Sandved); **E. Melanie Watt**: page 15.

Every reasonable effort has been made to trace ownership and to obtain permission to reprint copyright material. The publishers would be pleased to have any errors or omissions brought to their attention so that they may be corrected in subsequent printings.

Contents

Introduction

Bald eagles are sometimes called the lions of the sky.

Opposite: This eagle is perched at the Chilkat River in Alaska. As many as 3,000 bald eagles gather at this spot each year to feed on salmon.

Bald eagles are among the largest and most powerful birds in the world. They are sometimes called the lions of the sky. In North America, they are second in size only to the California condor. Eagles are a symbol of strength in many different cultures, yet there is much more to the bird than power.

In this book you will learn about the four different groups of eagles. You will find out where the expression "eagle-eyed" comes from. You will learn what bald eagles eat and how they hunt. You will also find out why you should never disturb a bald eagle when it is sitting on its nest.

Some populations of bald eagles began declining in the 1800s. Although most of these are now recovering, their troubles are not over. **Pesticides** and other pollutants are slowly poisoning the bald eagle's habitat. Read on, and find out why this is happening and how it affects the eagles.

Only a mature eagle has a completely white head and tail feathers.

Features

Bald eagles are not really bald.

Opposite: Despite their graceful appearance, bald eagles can be awkward flyers without perfect wind conditions.

Eagles are divided into four groups: snake eagles, buzzardlike eagles, booted eagles, and sea and fish eagles. The bald eagle belongs to the last group. The golden eagle, the other North American eagle, is a booted eagle.

Sea and fish eagles prey mostly on aquatic animals. They have long **talons**, or claws, and spiky knobs on their toes. These features help them to hold on to slippery prey.

Bald eagles are not really bald. Instead, their heads are covered with white feathers. The bald eagle's scientific name, *Haliaeetus leucocephalus*, actually means "white-headed sea eagle." We call the eagle "bald" after the word "piebald." Piebald describes markings that are two colors— usually black and white.

Golden eagles have feathers farther down their legs than bald eagles. They are called booted eagles because of these feathers.

Classification

Eagles are **raptors**, or birds of prey. This means that they eat other animals to survive. There are two main orders of raptors: the Strigiformes and the Falconiformes. The Strigiformes order includes all owls. These birds hunt mostly at night. The Falconiformes order includes eagles, vultures, hawks, falcons, osprey, and the secretary bird. They hunt mostly during the day. There are 56 species of eagles in the world. Of these, there are ten different kinds of sea and fish eagles.

If an eagle's feathers get too wet, it cannot take off from the water and may drown.

SEA AND FISH EAGLES OF THE WORLD

Species	Latin Name	Where They Live
African fish eagle	*Haliaeetus vocifer*	Africa
Bald eagle	*Haliaeetus leucocephalus*	North America
Pallas' sea eagle	*Haliaeetus leucoryphus*	Central Asia
Sanford's sea eagle	*Haliaeetus sanfordi*	Solomon Islands
Steller's sea eagle	*Haliaeetus pelagicus*	Siberia, Korea, Japan
White-bellied sea eagle	*Haliaeetus leucogaster*	Asia, Philippines, Indonesia, New Guinea, Australia
Madagascar fish eagle	*Haliaeetus vociferoides*	Madagascar
White-tailed sea eagle	*Haliaeetus albicilla*	Siberia, Norway, British Isles
Lesser fishing eagle	*Ichthyophaga nana*	South Asia, Indonesia
Gray-headed fishing eagle	*Ichthyophaga ichthyaectus*	South Asia, Malay Archipelago

Size

The size of a bald eagle can vary, depending on its age, gender, and where it lives. Immature eagles are often larger than adults. This is because a young eagle's tail and wing feathers are longer. Despite these longer feathers, immature eagles weigh less than adults.

As with most birds of prey, the females are larger than the males. There are many possible reasons for this. Some biologists believe that the larger size helps females defend their nest, eggs, and young. The smaller males can maneuver more easily, so they are better able to defend their territory. Female bald eagles have a wingspan of 7.5 feet (2.3 m). Males have a wingspan of only 6 feet (1.8 m).

Climate can affect an eagle's size. Bald eagles living in the colder parts of their range are larger than those living in warmer areas. A larger size gives eagles more strength to survive in colder, harsher climates.

LIFE SPAN

Bald eagles in captivity have lived for almost 50 years, but wild eagles probably have a much shorter life span. Wild eagles are vulnerable to disease and starvation. In addition, eagles often die when they come into contact with humans or human settlements. Wild eagles may be electrocuted by power lines, hit by vehicles, shot by hunters, or poisoned by pesticides.

Eyes and Vision

Vision is a bald eagle's most important sense. Birds have the best color vision of all animals. The resolution, or clarity, of a bald eagle's vision is exceptional, even better than its color vision. Eagles can see up to three times more clearly than humans. This is why we refer to sharp-sighted people as "eagle-eyed." Bald eagles' excellent vision allows them to see hidden prey better. Where we might see only a hump of beige fur, a bald eagle will be able to see five distinctly colored ground squirrels.

An eagle's excellent vision is partly due to its large eyes. An eagle's eyes are so big that there is little room for eye muscles to move its eyes around. To make up for this, eagles have many neck bones that make their necks very flexible. An eagle can turn its head in a 270-degree arc— three quarters of a circle around!

Like many other birds, bald eagles have a special eyelid on each eye called a **nictitating membrane**. This eyelid helps keep the eye moist and protects it from the wind. The membrane also reduces the glare from the sun.

Bald eagles have a bony eyebrow ridge that gives them a fierce appearance. Like the nictitating membrane, this ridge helps shield the eagle's eyes from the sun and protect them from dust and wind. It also guards its eyes from twigs or branches that may snap up when the bird flies down to perch in a tree. In addition, the ridge helps protect the eagle's eyes from struggling prey.

An eagle can spot a rabbit from half a mile (.8 km) away, and can judge how fast it must fly to catch its prey.

The rough bumps on the underside of an eagle's foot are called spicules. A bald eagle's spicules help it hold on to fish.

Feet, Talons, and Beak

Bald eagles have very strong feet that they use for capturing and killing prey. The undersides of their feet are rough like sandpaper. This helps the eagle hold on to slippery prey, such as fish or snakes. Compared to their body size, bald eagles also have quite large feet—up to 6 inches (15 cm) long!

Bald eagles have four toes, three in front and one behind. On the tips of their toes, they have long, curved talons. These razor-sharp talons are an eagle's most important weapon—they are even more dangerous than the raptor's hooked beak. The hind toe and talon are the most powerful. When a bald eagle grasps its prey, the hind talon digs deep into the victim, often piercing a vital organ, such as a heart or lung. The hind talon of a bald eagle is 2.8 to 3.2 inches (7 to 8 cm) long along its curve.

Like other birds, bald eagles have no teeth. They must swallow their food in pieces. They use their huge hooked beaks to tear up prey into bite-sized morsels. If the prey has not already been killed by the eagle's talons, it can be finished off with a sharp jab from the bird's beak.

Special Adaptations

Bald eagles have certain features that they share with other flying birds. These adaptations make it possible for the birds to fly.

Skeleton

Bald eagles have a thin, hollow skeleton with air-filled spaces. Many of the eagle's bones are fused, or joined, which makes them very strong. This kind of skeleton helps to support the raptors as they fly. An eagle's skeleton weighs less than half of what the eagle's feathers weigh.

Feathers

Bald eagles have feathers made up of a central shaft with many branches, or barbs. Each barb has hundreds of tiny hooks that stick to one another. The feather is strong as long as the barbs stay locked together by the hooks. Feathers help to support the eagle when it flies. Feathers also keep the eagle dry by shedding moisture.

Primary feathers are the long main feathers on a bird's wing. They are located from the tip of the wing to the bird's wrist. When eagles soar, gaps are visible between each primary feather. Eagles can adjust the size of these gaps while soaring to make precise movements or to keep a steady flight pattern. Sometimes eagles will also spread their long tail feathers to help steer their flight.

Like other soaring birds, bald eagles have specially adapted primary feathers. When held a certain way, these primaries form gaps that allow the eagles to better control their flight.

Eagles will perch where other birds can see them. This helps them defend their territory without fighting. Their distinctive plumage will warn other birds to stay away.

Plumage and Preening

A bird's covering of feathers is known as its plumage. Bald eagles have a unique plumage. An adult bald eagle has a bright white head and tail that stand out against its dark brown body. An immature bald eagle's plumage is a speckled combination of brown, tan, gray, black, and white.

Keeping its feathers in prime condition is essential for an animal that must rely on flight to survive. Bald eagles spend a large part of their day cleaning and taking care of their feathers. This behavior is called **preening**. During the preening process, an eagle removes damaged or old feathers. It combs its other feathers through its beak to reattach barbs and barbules that may have become separated. Preening is especially important for young eagles as they get their new plumage.

Bald eagles have a special gland located at the base of their tail. When pressed, this gland releases an oily liquid that the eagle spreads over its feathers. This oil helps waterproof the feathers and keep them in place. Once the bird has finished combing and cleaning its feathers, it shakes itself vigorously, shaking out any loose feathers and settling the others into place. A thorough preening can take a long time. A healthy adult bald eagle has over 7,000 feathers.

Social Life

Biologists believe winter gatherings may provide a place for young adult eagles to meet potential mates.

Opposite: A group of bald eagles takes a rest from feeding during the fall run of dog salmon in southeast Alaska.

Eagle pairs will often sit facing different directions to keep a lookout for prey.

How much bald eagles socialize depends upon the time of year. Adult eagles are busy with nesting activities in the spring and summer. During this time, breeding pairs stay close to their own territory. They rarely interact with other bald eagles, except to chase off intruders. Eagles that are too young to mate spend the warmer months exploring, learning about their environment, and trying to survive.

In the winter, and during **migration**, bald eagles are more sociable. Large groups of eagles often gather together around an abundant food source. Biologists believe these winter gatherings may provide a place for young adult eagles to meet potential mates.

Fall and Winter Social Activities

In the winter, bald eagles are less active than they are during the summer nesting season. A low activity level helps them conserve energy during the colder weather. Over 90 percent of their day is spent sleeping or dozing in the sun. The remaining time is spent looking for food and eating.

Group Feeding

Bald eagles find food in two ways—by foraging and by watching to see where other eagles are gathering. When many eagles gather or circle around one area, other eagles know that food is available there. A bald eagle can see a circling group from as far away as 40 miles (64 km). In this way, a bald eagle may be able to get a meal without using up a lot of energy trying to find it. Stealing another eagle's food is common. The best example of group feeding occurs on the Chilkat River, in Alaska. In the autumn and early winter, salmon lay eggs and die in this river. Many eagles gather to feast on their remains. More than 3,000 bald eagles have been seen in a 36-mile (60-km) stretch of the river.

Eagles will sometimes fish or bathe together in large groups.

Although eagles will roost together, they are careful to space themselves out. Roosts can be noisy as the birds defend their own space.

Roosting Together

During the winter, groups of eagles spend the night close together on **roosts**, or perching trees. Two birds may roost together in a tree, or more than 500 may roost in a small group of trees. Often the same roosting sites are used year after year.

There is quite a bit of shuffling around at a roosting site. If one eagle lands too close to another, the perched eagle will hiss and threaten the newcomer. If the new eagle is larger or older than the other, it may displace the smaller, younger bird. The displaced eagle then tries to find another perch. It may try to push out another eagle from its perch. The whole process can begin again with each new arrival. This kind of jostling continues until each eagle is comfortable, or until night falls.

In the morning, the eagles often leave the roosting site, one after another. They gather again at a feeding site. By following older, more experienced eagles, young, inexperienced eagles learn where to find food.

Communication

Bald eagles communicate with one another in a variety of ways. They make and respond to a number of different calls. In addition, visual displays play an important role in communication.

Calling

Bald eagles make many distinct sounds, ranging from a harsh cry to a low, snickering call. Eagles call to greet a mate or warn off intruders. Young eagles make a peeping or whining call to beg for food from their parents. When eagles gather in the winter, they are often quite vocal, especially when they have hunted successfully or stolen another eagle's dinner.

An eagle will try to protect its territory or prey with a high-pitched threat call.

Visual Displays

Visual displays are an essential part of eagle communication. An eagle defending its territory will chase or circle over an intruder until it leaves the area. If an eagle spots another that is feeding, it may raise its wings and talons, engaging in a mock attack to try to chase the other bird from its food. By far the most impressive visual displays are related to courtship.

Courtship displays take place each breeding season—even between birds that have been mated for a long time. One of the ways in which the birds court is by flight displays. One eagle may perform a roller-coaster display, flying up and down in a continuous motion like a roller coaster. In the cartwheel display, a courting pair begin by flying up very high. Then one eagle positions itself upside down beneath the other. The two eagles lock talons and begin to roll, first one on top, then the other. The entire time, they beat their wings to slow their fall. Just before reaching the ground, they separate and begin again. Eagles may tumble for several thousand feet (meters) in this fashion.

Naturalists Talk About Bald Eagles

Dr. Scott Nielsen

"For a season I was privileged to live with a pair of bald eagles...watching as they courted, built a home, and raised a family with a tenderness and caring entirely at odds with my preconceived notions."

Dr. Scott Nielsen is a bird biologist and photographer. His photographs have appeared in many North American nature publications, calendars, posters, and books. He is the author of *A Season with Eagles,* which he wrote after spending a season watching and photographing an eagle pair raise its family.

Dr. Mark Stalmaster

"Some condemn [the bald eagle] for its destructive powers; others consider it an unworthy symbol of the United States because of its 'decadent' lifestyle; many regard it with special pride because it symbolizes freedom and independence. Still others, especially those fortunate enough to have seen a wild eagle, appreciate it as an important component of a natural ecosystem."

Dr. Mark Stalmaster was a park ranger before becoming a wildlife biologist. He has worked with bald eagles for many years, observing them and raising them in captivity. He is the author of *The Bald Eagle.*

Priscilla Tucker

"For more than two hundred years, the bald eagle has symbolized the powerful freedom that is the United States of America. And for most of those two hundred years, the very people who have enjoyed the freedom of living in the United States have shot and poisoned the eagle, eliminated its winter food sources, and encroached on its nesting habitat."

Priscilla Tucker is a naturalist and former executive editor of the magazine *Birding.*

Eaglets

Bald eagles that live in more northern areas must worry about cold instead of heat when nesting.

Opposite: Eagles will often build their nests in the tallest trees available. This helps them watch for danger.

The mating season of bald eagles occurs at different times of the year, depending on where the birds live. In Arizona, eagles build nests and lay their eggs in September. In Texas and Florida, bald eagles nest in November or December. By nesting at these times, the eagles make sure their eaglets will not hatch during the hottest part of the year.

Bald eagles that live in more northern areas must worry about cold instead of heat when nesting. Eagles in northern Canada and Alaska often do not nest until mid-May, after the coldest weather has passed. If eggs are laid too early in these areas, the embryos may freeze.

A young eaglet will gain up to 4 ounces (113 g) of weight in a single day.

21

The Eyrie

A bald eagle's ideal nesting site must have a number of features, including a good view of the surrounding area, open areas for clear flight paths, close access to water, and a good site for the nest, or **eyrie**. A mated pair often returns to the same nest each season, reinforcing it and building it higher every year.

Bald eagles in California may nest on top of giant cacti, while eagles in the treeless Aleutian Islands of Alaska, nest on the ground. Eagles that live in forested areas prefer to build their eyries in large, sturdy trees. Bald eagles rarely build a nest at the very top of a tree because the branches are not strong enough to hold its weight. An old, well-established eyrie may weigh up to 2 tons (1,814 kg). Eagles usually build a nest about 80 feet (24.4 m) from the ground on a forked branch about 20 feet (6 m) from the top of the tree.

Both male and female eagles help build the nest. They use sticks, dead branches, grasses, cattails, mosses, and other plant material. A new nest

takes about one week to complete. If the eagles are fixing up an old nest, it takes them only a few days to finish.

A typical nest is about 4.8 to 6 feet (1.5 to 1.8 m) in diameter and 2.4 to 3.9 feet (.7 to 1.2 m) tall. However, if an eyrie is used over many generations, it can be much larger. One nest in Florida was 20 feet (6 m) high and almost 10 feet (3 m) wide!

Eagles will use sticks up to 7 feet (2.1 m) long to build their nests.

The Eggs

Once the eyrie is finished and the eagles have mated, the female becomes sluggish as eggs form inside her. This period of inactivity usually lasts for about one week, including egg-laying. During this time, the male eagle brings food to his mate.

Bald eagles may lay one to four eggs, but two are most common. Northern eagles often lay more eggs than do their southern cousins. Bald eagle eggs are dull white and weigh about 3.8 to 4.5 ounces (109 to 130 g). They measure 2.3 to 3.4 inches (5.8 to 8.6 cm) in length and 1.9 to 2.5 inches (4.8 to 6.3 cm) in width. The eggs are laid two to four days apart. The first egg is usually the largest and heaviest.

Until all the eggs are laid, the female eagle stays on the nest. When she is finished laying her eggs, both parents take turns sitting on the eggs to keep them warm. This warmth **incubates** the eggs. Incubating eagles

sit very low in the nest, using their bodies as shields to protect the eggs from predators and from extreme weather conditions.

The eggs are incubated for about 35 days. Because they are not laid at the same time, the eggs usually hatch a few days apart. When the eggs are almost ready to hatch, the eagles start to sit higher in the nest. Biologists think the eagles do this because they can sense movement within the eggs and do not want to squash an emerging eaglet.

Eagles are fiercely protective of their nests. They are even capable of knocking human intruders out of a tree.

Care

Newly hatched eaglets are completely dependent on their parents for food and protection. For the first few weeks, the parents spend all their time taking care of their young.

Brooding

Although young eaglets are born with a coat of soft, fluffy feathers called **down**, they cannot keep themselves warm. One of the parents must crouch down in the nest, keeping the young birds warm beneath its body and protecting them from rain, wind, or cold weather. This behavior is known as **brooding**. Parent eagles must brood their young for at least one month. After this time, the eaglets will have grown a second coat of down, and they will be able to keep themselves warm.

Defense

Eagle parents must be on guard against predators or other threats to the eaglets. Owls or other eagles will prey on a helpless eaglet if they get a chance. The parent eagles often sit by the nest facing in opposite directions. In this way, they can keep an eye on the entire area surrounding their nest.

Until young eagles fly, they must depend on their parents for food and protection.

Feeding

Feeding hungry eaglets is almost a full-time job. When the young eaglets squeal and peep in a food-begging call, the parents are quick to bring food to the nest. Parents rip the prey into small pieces, and the eaglets gobble them up. Feedings take place every 3 to 4 hours. After 6 or 7 weeks, the parents' job gets easier because the eaglets are able to rip prey apart by themselves.

Imprinting and Bonding

Bald eagles may desert their nest if they are disturbed—especially if they are disturbed by humans. Sometimes the nest contains eggs. The eagle parents desert the nest because they have not yet bonded with their young. Their instinct to flee from danger is stronger than their instinct to stay and guard the nest. Bonding takes place as the parents feed and care for their young eaglets. It usually occurs during the first two weeks after the young hatch. After this time, nest desertion is unlikely.

Newly hatched eaglets go through a process known as **imprinting**. Within a few days of hatching, young bald eagles imprint on the sight and sound of their parents. They do not recognize their parents specifically. Instead, they learn to identify the adults as their own kind. Once an eaglet has imprinted on its parents, it will accept food from any other bald eagle.

Imprinting is an important part of an eagle's life. By recognizing and watching others of its kind, an eaglet learns how to behave like an eagle and survive in its environment. When young bald eagles are ready to mate, they will look for partners that resemble their parents.

Imprinting ensures that bald eagles will seek other bald eagles as their partners.

Development

An eagle's nictitating membrane protects its eyes from accidental pecks by eager chicks.

Eaglets

A newly hatched eaglet does not look anything like its parents. Its eyes are closed, and its head wobbles around on a neck that seems too thin. A young eaglet's bare legs are pink. The rest of it is covered with down. After about 4 hours, it will open its eyes for the first time. A newly hatched eaglet weighs about 2.5 to 3.7 ounces (70 to 105 g).

After about 3 weeks, the soft gray down is replaced by thicker, longer, darker-colored down. The eaglet's legs turn bright yellow, and its beak darkens to a bluish-black. Unlike its yellow-eyed parents, a young eaglet has dark brown eyes. The eaglet grows rapidly, putting on about 4 ounces (113 g) of weight each day. By three weeks of age, the young bird weighs about 5 pounds (2.3 kg) and is 1 foot (30 cm) high.

Over the next few weeks, the eaglet's immature plumage starts to grow in, and the eaglet continues to grow quickly. Eaglets often squabble with one another over food. By this time they are able to tear up the prey their parents bring them. They also shuffle around the nest, building up strength in their legs. As their down is replaced by stronger feathers, the eaglets look rather ragged and messy. They preen often, learning how to take care of their feathers.

Fledglings

Bald eagles **fledge,** or learn to fly, 8 to 14 weeks after hatching. Most fledge at about 10 weeks. By this time, the young birds weigh about 11 pounds (5 kg). This is almost their full adult weight.

As the eaglets' juvenile feathers grow in, the young birds become more active around the nest. They practice their hunting skills by jumping on imaginary prey. They play by taking sticks away from each other, or by throwing twigs in the air and catching them in their talons. They also strengthen their flight muscles by flapping their wings.

Sometimes, during all this activity, an unfledged eaglet may tumble from the nest. Eaglets often spend their last few flightless days on the ground or perched on a low branch. When this happens, the parents bring food to their youngster until it fledges.

Male eaglets usually fledge a few days earlier than females. For the first few weeks after fledging, the young eagles practice their new skills close to the nest site. They still rely on their parents to bring them food, but they also begin to forage for themselves. After 6 to 10 weeks, they begin to leave the nest site and make their own way in the world. Bald eagles go through four stages, or **molts**, of immature plumage before they grow their adult plumage. The eagles get their adult plumage between four and five years of age. At this time, they are ready to mate.

Eagles will often fight in the nest. They can peck at each other's heads so hard that they will fall over.

Habitat

Wherever eagles live, they are never far from a river or shoreline.

Opposite: Perching is an energy-saving method of hunting. Eagles will watch the ground or water for hours, waiting to spot their prey.

Bald eagles like to live near water. They live along seacoasts, beside lakes and rivers, or even in swamplands. Wherever eagles live, they are never far from a river or shoreline.

Bald eagle habitats usually include two specific kinds of areas. They need a foraging area where food is consistent and plentiful. The area must also include open spaces, such as beaches and sandbars, where prey can be killed and eaten.

A good perching area is also important. When an eagle perches in an exposed area, it is letting others know the territory is occupied. A perching area may include tall trees, rocks, cliffs, logs, ice, or even fence posts and poles. These are places where eagles can rest, stand guard, or watch for prey.

Bald eagles live near their favorite prey—fish.

Eagle Territories

Bald eagles have three levels of territories: the nest site, the breeding territory, and the home range. A home range is the area where eagles search for food. Its size depends on the amount of food that is available and on the number of other eagles in the area. In general, home ranges are a minimum of 4 to 6 square miles (10 to 15 sq km). Ranges are larger in places where food and other bald eagles are scarce. Bald eagles do not defend their home ranges.

Breeding territories are a different matter. Bald eagles will defend their territory against any intruders. A territory is about .4 to .8 square miles (1 to 2 sq km) in size, but is often long and narrow. Because they are fishing birds, water is more important to bald eagles than land. As a result, their territories often stretch along the length of a river or shoreline. The nest site is located within a bald eagle's territory.

An eagle's territory is usually much smaller in the winter months, when it must stay near locations with unfrozen water.

Soaring Eagles

When the sun shines on Earth, masses of warm air rise in columns or currents known as **thermals**. Bald eagles ride these thermals by stretching their wings and soaring upward. **Updrafts** occur when steady winds blow against a hill or mountainside and force air upward. Bald eagles also take advantage of these rising pockets of air. When riding a thermal or updraft, an eagle appears to fly gracefully and effortlessly. However, if there are no rising columns of air, a bald eagle's flight often appears awkward and clumsy.

Bald eagles soar on a thermal or updraft by holding their wings straight out or in a slight V shape. A good thermal can carry a bald eagle as high as 6,500 feet (1,980 m). When the rising air column breaks up, the eagle glides downward and forward. In this way, bald eagles can travel for great distances while using little energy. When migrating, a bald eagle may travel up to 270 miles (435 km) in a single day.

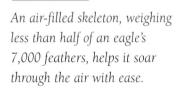

An air-filled skeleton, weighing less than half of an eagle's 7,000 feathers, helps it soar through the air with ease.

Migration

Migration is a regular seasonal movement from a winter range to a summer range, and back again. Most eagle populations migrate north in late winter or early spring. In the fall, they migrate south. Some bald eagles that live in warmer southern areas do not migrate at all. Instead, they live in the same region all year-round. Others migrate north in mid- to late summer, then back south in the fall. The bald eagles that do migrate usually fly between the same summer and winter ranges each year.

Spring migration

During spring migration, bald eagles travel later in the day than they do during fall migration. The reason for this has to do with the availability of thermals. In the spring, thermals are at their best in the late afternoon. In many western states and provinces, spring weather conditions are often poor. This makes flight more difficult for bald eagles. As a result, the eagles must move quickly, so they take full advantage of late afternoon thermals.

A bald eagle's wingspan can be over 7 feet (2.1 m) wide.

Fall migration

Biologists believe that fall migration is triggered by food supply. As long as there is enough food, eagles prefer to stay where they are. Cold weather is not a problem—bald eagles can live in very low temperatures. For eagles living in northern areas, problems arise when waterfowl, a favorite prey, begin to migrate south. The situation worsens when rivers and streams freeze over and bald eagles cannot get at the fish. Without fish or waterfowl, the eagles are left with few food sources. As food becomes scarce, bald eagles head south.

Fall migration takes place mainly during October and November. Bald eagles almost always migrate alone. Even mated pairs split up to make the journey. The eagles usually begin to migrate in the late morning or early afternoon. They often continue until dusk. If the weather becomes snowy or overcast, eagles will often wait until it clears before continuing on their way.

Younger eagles are usually the first to head south in the fall and the last to arrive on the winter ground. Unfamiliar with the routes and landmarks, they often wander off course. Some may even die of starvation if they are unable to find a good wintering spot.

Bald eagles can live in cold temperatures. They migrate only if they cannot find food.

How to Spot a Bald Eagle

Other North American raptors can be easily mistaken for bald eagles. Learn the following characteristics so you can tell them apart:

Bald eagles

An adult bald eagle's size and striking colors make it easy to identify. Just look for the distinctive white head and tail against a dark brown body. It is a little more difficult to identify immature bald eagles. They are speckled, often with patches of white on their wings, breast, back, head, and tail. Bald eagles live near bodies of water.

Golden eagles

A golden eagle is almost as large as a bald eagle. Its head and body are dark brown with a wash of gold on the back of the neck. An immature golden eagle looks similar to an immature bald eagle, but the bald eagle shows more white on the feathers at the base of the primaries. Golden eagles prefer mountainous habitats.

Ospreys

An osprey is smaller than a bald eagle. The two birds occupy similar habitats. One way to tell an osprey apart from a bald eagle is to look at the bird's breast and head. An osprey has a white breast and a black patch on each cheek. Another way to tell the two apart is by the shape of their wings in flight. A bald eagle's wings appear straighter than the osprey's more bent wings.

A bald eagle may be living in the area if you can see...

1. A large bird circling high in the air.

2. A bald eagle perched on a tree, cliff, or other exposed area.

3. A large nest, made out of sticks, in the shape of a cylinder, bowl, cone, or disk.

4. White splotches of feces on the ground at the foot of a large tree or cliff. This "whitewash" accumulates over time and is very easy to see from a distance.

5. A stray feather caught in the branches of a possible perching tree.

6. Masses of compact feathers, fur, or bones lying on the ground beneath a perching site. Like owls, bald eagles cough up tube-shaped masses of the parts of their prey that could not be digested. These masses are known as **pellets**.

Eagles are said to build the "mansions" of North American bird nests.

Food

A bald eagle's diet consists of fish, birds, and mammals.

Opposite: Eagles often find an easy meal in carrion.

Bald eagles are both hunters and scavengers. Their ability to eat many things helps them survive in an environment where prey may sometimes be difficult to find. A bald eagle's diet consists of fish, birds, and mammals. They like to eat fish the best. Their favorite fish are those that swim near the surface of the water. These fish are easy to see and catch.

Waterfowl, such as geese and ducks, are also a favorite prey item. Bald eagles will hunt just about any kind of waterbird or seabird, especially if the bird is injured or sick. They like to eat mammals least. Eagles kill and eat smaller mammals, such as mice, muskrats, and squirrels. They also scavenge the meat off larger mammals, such as deer or seals, that have died from other causes. These dead animals are called **carrion**. In one case, bald eagles were even seen eating a dead sperm whale that had washed up onto shore.

Eagles have strong beaks that help them transport their prey to a good spot to eat. Sometimes eagles will eat small prey while flying.

Hunting and Foraging

Although it is possible for a healthy bald eagle to go for a week without food, eagles usually eat about 6 to 11 percent of their body weight each day. They need more food in the winter because they use more energy to keep warm. An eagle's stomach is rather small. When it finds or captures a large amount of food, it stores some of the food in a pouch halfway between its mouth and its stomach. This pouch is called a **crop**. A full-grown eagle can store about 32.6 ounces (924 g) of food in its crop. This feature allows the eagle to store food for times when prey is scarce.

Bald eagles have several hunting and foraging techniques. They prefer to eat whatever is available with the least amount of effort. Stealing food from others is a favorite strategy. Bald eagles steal fish from osprey in midair and chase vultures away from carrion. Eagles will even swoop down on a sea otter, snatching the otter's meal right off its belly.

Like vultures, bald eagles are always on the lookout for a meal of carrion. In the winter, this kind of scavenging is more common because fishing opportunities are limited and other prey are hard to find.

Bald eagles hunt when they cannot steal or scavenge. An eagle flies above water or along the shoreline looking for prey. Once the eagle spots its prey, it drops down quickly with its talons extended. This is called **stooping**. Eagles kill fish, waterfowl, and mammals with their talons. Sometimes a fish may be too large for an eagle to lift in the air. When this happens, the eagle flaps its wings and swims awkwardly to shore, towing its catch in its talons.

To catch a fish, an eagle stoops to the surface of the water.

The Food Web

Each living thing pictured below belongs to a food chain. A food chain shows how energy, in the form of food, is passed from one living thing to another. The arrows point to the direction in which the energy is transferred. For example, microscopic animals are food for fish, which are food for a bald eagle. Every animal survives by eating plants or animals in its food chain.

A food web is made up of many food chains. As you can see from this food web, bald eagles belong to many food chains. How many food chains would be affected if bald eagles disappeared?

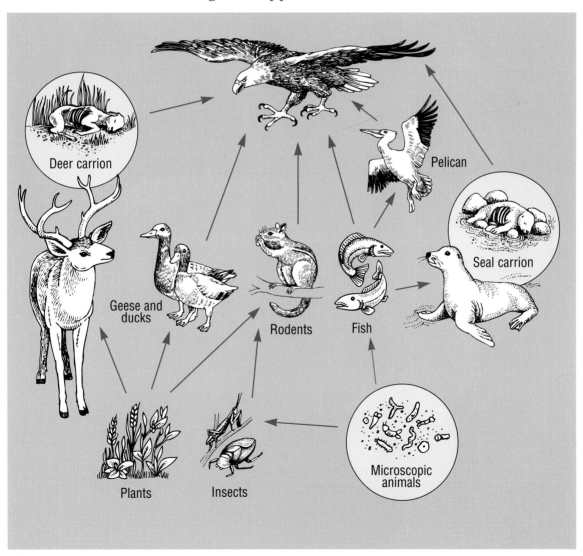

Deer carrion

Pelican

Seal carrion

Geese and ducks

Rodents

Fish

Plants

Insects

Microscopic animals

Competition

As human populations have grown and spread, bald eagles have lost much of their traditional habitat.

Opposite: Eagles trying to steal food from other eagles have to deal with their opponent's sharp beak.

Bald eagles usually dominate the feeding at a food carcass.

Adult bald eagles are so large and powerful that they usually win any competition with other birds. Other predators and scavengers also look for food at salmon runs and spawning pools, but bald eagles win a good portion of the dead fish.

By far, a bald eagle's worst enemies are humans. As human populations have grown and spread, bald eagles have lost much of their traditional habitat. The land that has not been converted to farms and cities has often been poisoned with pesticides and other pollutants.

Competing with Other Bald Eagles

Bald eaglets compete with each other while they are still in the nest. Eaglets compete aggressively for food with their siblings. Although one researcher has observed bald eagle parents preventing their eaglets from fighting, this discipline is not common.

Adult bald eagles often compete with one another for food. A larger, heavier eagle is quick to snatch a meal away from a smaller eagle. Sometimes the two will scuffle a bit, each trying to hold on to a piece of the prey. Other times the two eagles may even lock talons. Aggressive bald eagles are more likely to chase off potential thieves.

Adult eagles may also compete with one another for nesting territory. Once a pair has established its territory, they advertise their presence by perching and by calling out to warn off other birds. Usually other eagles avoid the established pair, so conflicts are rare. If another eagle does venture into an established territory, the mated pair will chase it off. Immature intruders are also chased away, but often not as aggressively.

If given a choice, eagles often prefer scavenging or stealing prey to hunting on their own.

Other birds can be very aggressive about stealing food from bald eagles. Observers have seen one raven pull at an eagle's feathers to distract it while another raven was stealing its food.

Relationships with Other Animals

Bald eagles compete with other birds and animals for food, and sometimes other birds or animals prey on eagles. Eagle eggs and newly hatched eaglets are very vulnerable to predators. These predators include seagulls, owls, gray squirrels, red squirrels, raccoons, and crows. Bald eagle parents must be on guard against these predators at all times.

Other animals will also try to steal food from bald eagles. A coyote may succeed in chasing an eagle away from a carcass. Sometimes crows and seagulls may steal small parts of a bald eagle's dinner. Most of the time, however, the eagle will not hesitate to punish a thief. In one case, an eagle killed a vulture that was trying to take off with its prey.

Competing with Humans

Eagles compete with humans for both food and territory. Most of the time, eagles lose the competition. Eagles need old forests with tall trees in which to build their nests. When settlers first moved to North America, many of these forests were cut down to make way for farms and cities. When this happened, eagles had little choice but to leave the area and try to find other nest sites.

In addition, eagles rely mainly on fish for their diet, but people also use this resource. As humans deplete fish stocks, eagles have a harder time finding enough food.

Another problem in eagle-human relationships has to do with waterfowl. Both eagles and humans hunt these waterbirds for food. Human hunters sometimes use lead shot in their guns. Lead shot is poisonous when it is dissolved. Sometimes birds that have been injured by lead shot are eaten by eagles. The lead shot then dissolves in the eagle's stomach acids, slowly poisoning the bird. Although lead shot has now been banned in many areas, some jurisdictions in North America still permit it.

Human presence in eagle territories can have unexpected and dangerous consequences.

The War Against Eagles

When Europeans first came to North America in the early 1600s, there were about 250,000 to 500,000 bald eagles in Canada and the United States. Many Aboriginal peoples revered the eagle, but Europeans saw the bird only as a pest and a competitor for food. Eagles preyed on the grouse, rabbits, and fish that the new settlers also hunted. In addition, many colonists believed that eagles preyed on livestock, such as cattle.

By the early 1800s, many counties offered bounties on dead eagles. In 1806, for example, a dead bald eagle was worth 20 cents in Knox County, Maine. Eagles were shot for money and sport. Eggs were collected and sold to museums and exhibits. Nesting trees were chopped down, and eaglets were taken from their nests. Under this assault, bald eagle populations declined sharply. Populations that lived in the interior of North America were most severely affected.

In 1893, a scientist examined the stomach contents of a number of bald eagles. He discovered that eagles preyed on mice, rats, snakes, and other pests, rather than on livestock. As a result of his findings, some people began calling for state protection for the birds. Some states signed laws protecting the bald eagle, but the laws were not easy to enforce. In addition, many hunters could not tell the difference between bald eagles and other raptors, so they just shot them all. Alaska continued to offer bounties on bald eagles until 1953.

Even today, the most common sources of death among bald eagles relate to human activity.

Folklore

Eagles are found in the folklore and legends of many different cultures. Some of the myths about eagles evolved from their biology. Since eagles are able to soar high in the sky, people associated eagles with the sun. The sun was also often linked to royalty. An eagle's presence was therefore believed to predict the birth of kings or other important royal events.

The presence of an eagle was not always a positive sign. People saw eagles soaring in the wind and began to link the birds with stormy weather. In some cultures, it was even believed that eagles caused the storms by flapping their wings. Also, eagles are often found around dead animals because they eat carrion. As a result of this, some ancient people believed that eagles were prophets of death.

Opposite: Zeus was the king of the gods in Greek mythology. His symbols included the thunderbolt and the eagle.

The eagle has often been associated with the sun and with royalty.

Spirit Eagles

The spirit eagle lives on the tallest mountains. It soars high in the heavens, far beyond the reach of humans. It is the king of all birds. Eagles have often been linked with the powers of the sky and the gods. In many cultures, eagles were thought to be messengers of the gods because they were so powerful and could fly so high.

Ancient Greeks believed the gods would not harm their own messengers with lightning. Eagles were tied to the roofs of Greek temples to prevent lightning from striking. Romans and Greeks also believed that eagles had healing power. In ancient times, eagle talons, feathers, and bones were often used to make medicines.

In ancient Babylon, the souls of rulers were believed to rise to heaven on an eagle. Whenever a ruler died, an eagle was released at the funeral so that the ruler's soul could rise to live with the gods.

Eagles are important in many North American Aboriginal cultures. In some, eagles are seen as messengers or symbols of the great spirit. As such, eagles are seen to have vision and strength. The eagle spirit is said to help heal those who are sick or injured.

Warrior Eagles

Eagles often symbolize strength, pride, and power. These are qualities that have been admired by warriors throughout history. As a result, the eagle has been a popular symbol with the military in many different times and places.

Ancient warriors used eagle feathers for making arrows. They believed that these arrows had the strength, speed, and skill of the eagle. Each Roman Legion carried a special pole topped with a golden eagle. The Muslim warrior Saladin had an eagle on his coat of arms. A special group of Aztec warriors was named "Eagles." Iroquois warriors wore eagle feathers to symbolize their bravery. Eagles have appeared on the shields and military uniforms of many different countries.

Eagles are also national emblems in many countries. In the United States, the bald eagle stands for power, independence, and victory over enemies. In Mexico, the national emblem is an eagle devouring a snake. This symbol of an eagle and snake appears in cultures from India, South and Central America, and New Zealand.

In folklore, snakes are usually symbols of evil, while eagles are symbols of good. An eagle killing a snake therefore symbolizes the battle between the forces of good and evil.

Folktales

Folktale eagles are usually intelligent, skilled, and helpful. They help people escape from enemies and teach them healing dances and ceremonies. There are many stories about eagles told in many different cultures. Here are a few you might enjoy:

How and Why Stories

The North American Yokuts tale **"The Lizard-Hand"** tells of the Eagle creator, his assistant Coyote, and how death came into the world.

Leach, Maria. *How the People Sang the Mountains Up*. New York: Viking, 1967.

In **"Ton and the Eagles,"** you will discover the origin of eagles with red-tipped wings.

Yellow Robe, Rosebud. *Tonweya and the Eagles and Other Lakota Folk Stories*. New York: Dial Press, 1979.

Foolish Eagles

In the Scottish folktale **"The Eagle and the Wren,"** a powerful eagle is fooled by a tiny wren during a flying contest.

Montgomerie, Norah. *Twenty-Five Fables*. New York: Abelard-Schuman, 1961.

Helpful Eagles

In one tale from this collection, a man runs from his enemies and seeks shelter in an eagle's nest. He learns the eagle's rites and ceremonies before defeating both his own and the eagles' enemies.

Brown, Dee. *Folktales of the American Indian*. New York: Holt, Rinehart, and Winston, 1993.

"The Flood" is an Inuit story about the Chief of Heaven, who sends a flood to Earth because he cannot sleep. As people escape in canoes, the eagles work out a way to make the waters recede.

Caswell, Helen. *Shadows from the Singing House*. Rutland: Tuttle, 1968.

In **"Waukewa's Eagle,"** a boy saves an injured eaglet that later rescues him from a canoe accident.

Hardendorff, Jeanne. *The Frog's Saddle Horse and Other Tales*. Philadelphia: Lippincott, 1969.

In **"The Cruel Uncle,"** the Eagle people help a young man overcome his cruel, murderous uncle. The man learns to become an eagle himself and drops his uncle into the sea.

Maher, Ramona. *The Blind Boy and the Loon, and Other Eskimo Myths*. New York: Day, 1969.

"Eagle Boy" tells the story of a kind boy who gives part of his catch to the eagles. When he and his brother are deserted by their people, the eagles help the boys by bringing them food.

Martin, Fran. *Nine Tales of Raven*. New York: Harper, 1951.

In a Chuckee tale from this collection, Eagle destroys the evil spirit Ke'let by carrying him up high and dropping him.

Newell, Edythe. *The Rescue of the Sun and Other Tales from the Far North*. Chicago: Albert Whitman, 1970.

Bald Eagle Distribution

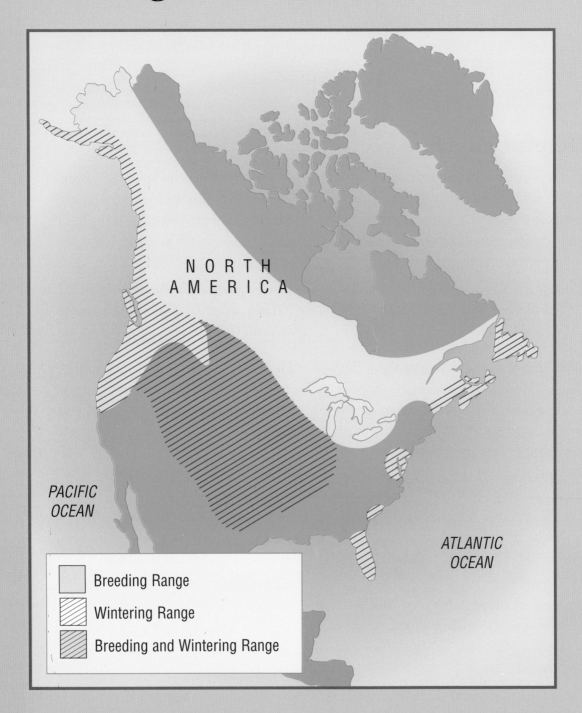

NORTH AMERICA

PACIFIC OCEAN

ATLANTIC OCEAN

Breeding Range

Wintering Range

Breeding and Wintering Range

Status

In 1940 the Bald Eagle Protection Act was passed in the United States.

Under the Bald Eagle Protection Act, people are allowed to use eagle parts for scientific, exhibition, and Aboriginal religious purposes.

A drop in bald eagle populations was first noticed in the late 1800s. Over the next few decades, many people became more concerned with the decline, especially because humans were mostly responsible for it. By 1921, an article in the magazine *Ecology* discussed the possible extinction of the bird. Despite the growing concern, bald eagles did not receive adequate protection until 1940. In that year, the Bald Eagle Protection Act was passed in the United States. Under this act, it is illegal to kill a bald eagle or to possess bald eagle feathers, talons, nests, or eggs. It is also against the law to disturb the eagles in any way. In 1952 the act was extended to include Alaska. From the 1950s to the mid-1960s, enforcement of the act was uneven. In Texas alone, 20,000 bald and golden eagles were shot by hired gunners.

Endangered Species Legislation

1940
Bald Eagle Protection Act made it illegal to kill or trade in the parts of bald eagles

1952
Bald Eagle Protection Act extended to include Alaska

1962
Bald Eagle Protection Act extended to include protection for golden eagles

1966
Endangered Species Preservation Act called for protection for all endangered U.S. wildlife, but gave few powers to do so

1973
Endangered Species Act (ESA) gave conservation legislation more power. Under the ESA, even a federal government department, such as the U.S. Department of Defense, must consult the Fish and Wildlife Service or the National Fisheries Service if its project may harm an endangered species.

Pesticides and Poisons

DDT is a pesticide that was first discovered and used in 1939. By the late 1940s, many people were using it because it was so effective at killing insects. In 1951, 106 million pounds (48 million kg) of DDT were used in the United States alone. As more and more DDT was released into the environment, insects began to develop immunities to the pesticide. Stronger and more deadly versions of the pesticide were invented. In the early 1950s, bald eagle populations were beginning to recover from human persecution. As the use of DDT became more widespread, eagle populations began to decline once again.

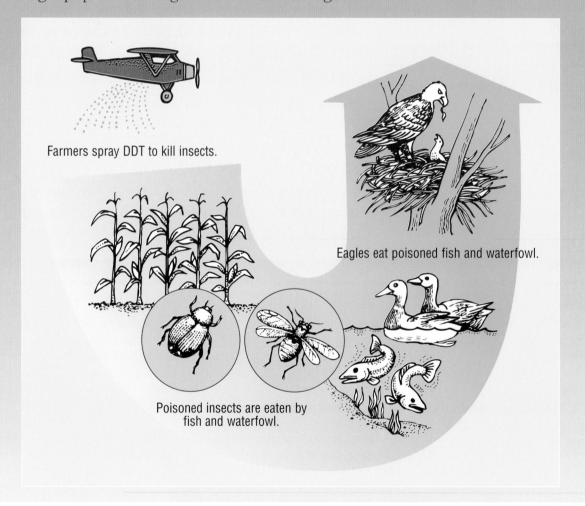

Farmers spray DDT to kill insects.

Eagles eat poisoned fish and waterfowl.

Poisoned insects are eaten by fish and waterfowl.

DDT breaks down slowly in the environment. Poisoned insects are eaten by fish and waterfowl, which are then eaten by eagles. The poisons in pesticides become more concentrated as they move up the food chain. By the time DDT reaches bald eagles, the pesticides are extremely toxic.

The Dangers of DDT

DDT blocked the production of calcium in adult eagles. Calcium is what makes eggshells thick and bones strong. As a result of DDT poisoning, many bald eagles laid eggs with shells that were too thin. The eggs often broke as the parent eagles incubated them. Even if the eggs did not break, the eaglets inside did not get enough calcium to make their bones strong. Sometimes eggs rotted without hatching at all. Eaglets that hatched from these eggs were weak or deformed. Many died soon after hatching. By 1970 only about 1,000 bald eagles were breeding successfully in the United States, not including Alaska.

In the late 1960s, people began to realize how DDT and other pesticides were affecting wildlife. Preserves were established to help protect some of the bald eagles' habitat. The use of DDT was restricted in Canada in 1970. In 1972 it was banned in the United States. However, because DDT breaks down so slowly, it is still in the environment. It is also carried by wind from other countries, such as Mexico, that continue to use it.

Many other chemicals are also harmful to bald eagles. Some of these have now been banned, but the problems with them are not yet over. The chemicals may take decades to break down. As they break down in the environment, they often form more toxic substances. These poisons also enter the food chain, causing deformity or death in bald eagle populations.

Bald eagle populations are recovering. In 1995 the eagles were moved from endangered to threatened status. However, the danger for bald eagles is not over. Chemical waste and garbage continues to poison bald eagles and other wildlife. Acid rain kills the fish that bald eagles eat. In many areas, the environment is no longer clean enough to support a bald eagle population. If bald eagles are to be saved, people must also save their habitats.

Viewpoints

Should countries continue to use chemical pesticides?

Agricultural pests include insects, bacteria, weeds, fungi, viruses, birds, rodents, and mammals. Chemical pesticides kill the pests and increase the amount of crops that farmers can harvest and sell.

PRO

1 Each year, 48 percent of the world's food crops are destroyed by pests. In a world with so many people, we cannot afford crop losses of this size.

2 Biological controls for pests include trapping or sterilizing male insects so they cannot breed. Unfortunately, these controls are not completely effective. Crops will continue to be destroyed if we rely only on biological controls.

3 Not all chemicals are harmful, as long as certain steps are taken. These steps include using small amounts of pesticides and applying them at the most effective time. Chemical pesticides should be used only to reduce the size of a pest population. Afterward, biological controls, which are less harmful to the environment, can be used to keep the population low.

CON

1 Chemical pesticides upset the balance of an ecosystem. For example, if pesticides kill one kind of insect, then that insect's competitors may grow in number. This growing population may then become a pest. When this happens, more pesticides will need to be released.

2 We now have other controls for insects and pests. By doing things like changing crops each year or controlling soil nutrients, farmers can control pests without using chemicals.

3 The harmful effects of pesticides have been proven by the example of bald eagles and DDT. However, wild creatures are not the only ones vulnerable to poisonous pesticides. Many pesticides are also harmful to humans. No matter how carefully a pesticide is used, it will still end up in the environment, where it can harm both people and wildlife.

Sponsorship

Many bald eagle experts believe that the future of bald eagles depends on how much people want to save them and their habitats. To help people better understand and appreciate bald eagles, biologists study the eagles and their populations. You can help them by sponsoring a bald eagle through HawkWatch International, Inc.

Many people have helped biologists study eagles by adopting a wild eagle.

HawkWatch International, Inc.

HawkWatch International is an organization that is dedicated to the conservation of raptors. Scientists at HawkWatch put leg bands on raptors so they can track the birds' movements and migrations. By keeping track of banded birds, scientists can also tell if a population consists of old birds, young birds, or a healthy mixture of both. Each year, biologists count the number of migrating eagles, hawks, falcons, and other raptors. All this information helps scientists identify and help threatened species. Problems can be identified before a species becomes endangered.

You can help by participating in HawkWatch's Adopt-A-Hawk program. In this program, you can adopt a wild bald eagle. You will receive a certificate with a color photo of a bald eagle as well as an information sheet about the weight, height, gender, and band number of your eagle. You will also find out when and where your eagle was banded. For more information about this program, write to:

HawkWatch International, Inc.
P.O. Box 6600
Salt Lake City, UT
84110-0660
e-mail: hawkwatch@charitiesusa.com

You can find out more about HawkWatch International on the Internet at:
http://www.vpp.com/HawkWatch/

What You Can Do

By learning more about bald eagles, you can make better decisions about how to help them. Write to a government organization, a conservation group, or a raptor rehabilitation center to get more information about these amazing birds.

Conservation Groups

UNITED STATES

The Raptor Research Foundation
James Fitzpatrick
Carpenter Nature Center
12805 St. Croix Trail
Hastings, MN
55033

The Raptor Center
1920 Firch Ave.
St. Paul, MN
55108

Institute for Wildlife Research
National Wildlife Federation
1400 16th St. NW
Washington, D.C.
20036

CANADA

Nature Conservancy Canada
4th floor, 110 Eglinton Ave. W.
Toronto, Ontario
M4R 2G5

Canadian Nature Federation
1 Nicholas St.
Suite 520
Ottawa, Ontario
K1N 7B7

Rehabilitation Centers

Bald eagles and other raptors may be injured in various ways, including colliding with power lines or fences. There are now many places in North America where these injured birds may be taken and helped. Many of these centers also offer educational programs or school visits. You can sometimes volunteer to look after the birds at some of these centers. Check your phone book to find a rehabilitation center near you.

Twenty Fascinating Facts

1 Eagles use branches and other plant material to build their nests. Sometimes they even use garbage. Biologists have found many strange items built into bald eagle nests, including plastic bottles, clothespins, lightbulbs, and golf balls.

2 Bald eagles build larger nests than any other bird in North America.

3 Bald eagles are bulky and heavy. As such, it is difficult for them to get off the ground if there are no thermals or updrafts. This can be dangerous for the eagles. Sometimes bald eagles feed on road-killed deer at the side of a highway. When vehicles pass by, the eagles sometimes cannot get off the ground fast enough to avoid being hit and killed by cars.

4 Bald eagles rely on their powerful feet and sharp talons for more than hunting. When defending itself on a nest, a bald eagle will sometimes lean back and try to rake intruders with its talons.

5 In Florida, some immature bald eagles migrate north during the winter. They do not go very far, but often meet up and mix with northern populations that have come south for the colder months.

6 Bald eagles spend a lot of time keeping their feathers clean and in order. Sometimes the eagles wade into shallow water and splash around, wetting their soiled feathers. They then fly to a nearby perch to dry off and preen.

7 In very old, large eyries, owls or mice may nest in the bottom areas while eagles nest on top.

8 Most bald eagles build more than one nest in their territory. Biologists do not know why they do this. One theory is that the eagle's building instinct is not satisfied after only one nest. Another theory is that the second nest is a kind of backup—ready to move into if the first is destroyed.

9 Bald eagles often build their nests high in trees. Sometimes the nest site can get very hot. When this happens, eagles can pant like a cat or dog to cool off.

10 After the eaglets hatch, the male eagle starts to bring fresh pine branches and other green plant material to the nest. Biologists are not sure why the eagles do this. The greenery may provide camouflage, protection from the sun, or it may simply help keep the nest clean and fresh.

11 During the incubation period, the eggshell slowly weakens. When an eaglet is ready to hatch, it will be able to peck its way out by using an egg tooth, a small rough knob on its beak. An eaglet's egg tooth falls off after about a month.

12 Nesting bald eagles develop a **brood patch**. This is a place on the stomach where the bird's feathers have fallen out. Direct contact with the bare skin of a brood patch keeps the eggs warmer.

13 Sometimes fishers lose their hooks and line when a fish gets away. If this fish is then caught by a bald eagle parent, the hook and line are brought to the nest inside the fish. Usually an eagle parent will pick out these dangerous bits before offering the fish to its eaglets. Fishhooks and fishing line can often be found beneath bald eagle nests.

14 A bald eagle can fly while carrying prey that weighs up to one-third its own weight. In many cases, however, an eagle will simply drag heavy prey to stable ground before eating it.

15 Immature eagles have longer feathers than adults. The reason for this is related to their diet. Younger eagles eat mostly carrion, while adult eagles often capture their own prey. Longer feathers are better for soaring and gliding in search of carrion. Shorter feathers are better for flying quickly and attacking.

16 Power lines kill many eagles. A bald eagle's wingspan is so large that the bird can touch two wires and get electrocuted.

17 It is very common for bald eagles to steal food from other animals. American statesman and scientist Benjamin Franklin was appalled when he discovered this. He thought that a bird of "such bad moral character" should not be his country's national symbol. Instead, he suggested that the wild turkey would make a better symbol.

18 In ten days, scientists once observed 45 bald eagles eating the complete remains of a dead whale that washed up onto shore.

19 In many cases, eagle parents have fought off biologists who were trying to study their eaglets. In Alaska, eagles have even been known to attack biologists' helicopters!

20 In most places, it is illegal to possess any bald eagle parts, but some American Aboriginal groups need eagle feathers or feet for their religious ceremonies. The National Eagle Repository is a department of the United States Fish and Wildlife Service. The Repository collects and distributes eagle parts to Native Americans for religious purposes.

Glossary

brooding: When a parent crouches down in the nest to cover the young and protect them from extreme weather

brood patch: A featherless patch on the underside of an eagle that allows warmth to pass from the bird's body to the eggs

carrion: The flesh of a dead animal

crop: An eagle's pouch, halfway between its mouth and stomach, where the bird can store food

down: A covering of soft, fluffy feathers

eyrie: An eagle's nest

fledge: To learn how to fly. It also means to acquire flight feathers.

imprinting: A process in which newly hatched birds form a strong bond to their parents

incubate: To sit on eggs in order to hatch them by the warmth of the body

migration: A regular, seasonal movement from a winter range to a summer range, and back again

molt: When a bird loses its feathers and replaces them with new ones

nictitating membrane: A bird's clear, third eyelid that keeps its eye moist and protects it from dust, wind, and sun

pellets: Small, dense masses that eagles cough up, consisting of the indigestible parts of their prey

pesticides: Chemicals used to kill plant or animal pests

preening: When a bird grooms itself by smoothing and straightening its feathers

raptors: Birds of prey

roosts: Perching trees where eagles spend the night

stooping: Dropping down quickly on prey with talons extended

talons: An eagle's long, curved claws

thermals: Columns, or currents, of warm air that rise up in the sky

updrafts: Rising air that occurs when steady winds blow against hills or mountainsides and force air up

Suggested Reading

Amato, Carol. *The Bald Eagle*. Hauppauge, New York: Barron's, 1996.

Boyer, Trevor. *Vanishing Eagles*. New York: Dragon's World, 1983.

Gerrard, Jon M., and Gary R. Bartolotti. *The Bald Eagle: Haunts and Habits of a Wilderness Monarch*. Saskatoon, Saskatchewan: Western Producer Prairie Books, 1988.

Nielson, Scott. *A Season with Eagles*. Stillwater: Voyageur Press, 1991.

Ryden, Hope. *America's Bald Eagle*. New York: P. Putnam's Sons, 1985.

Savage, Candace. *Eagles of North America*. Saskatoon, Saskatchewan: Western Producer Prairie Books, 1987.

Stalmaster, Mark. *The Bald Eagle*. New York: Universe Books, 1987.

Tucker, Priscilla. *The Return of the Bald Eagle*. Mechanicsburg, Pennsylvania: Stackpole Books, 1994.

Index